T0324008

BEIT

Eryn Green

New Issues Poetry & Prose

A Green Rose Book

New Issues Poetry & Prose
The College of Arts and Sciences
Western Michigan University
Kalamazoo, Michigan 49008

First Edition, 2020.

ISBN: 978-1-936970-66-7 (paperbound)

Library of Congress Cataloging-in-Publication Data:
Green, Eryn
BEIT/Eryn Green
Library of Congress Catalog Card Number: 2019055290

Editor:	Nancy Eimers
Managing Editor:	Kimberly Kolbe
Associate Editors:	Alyssa Jewell & Connor Yeck
Art Direction:	Nicholas Kuder
Design:	Victoria Tomasello
Production:	Paul Sizer
	The Design Center, Frostic School of Art
	College of Fine Arts
	Western Michigan University
Printing:	McNaughton & Gunn, Inc.

BEIT

Eryn Green

New Issues

WESTERN MICHIGAN UNIVERSITY

Also by Eryn Green

Eruv

For Hanna and Aya—my beit, my bet

Contents

"*He who walks with his house on his head is heaven.*"
—Charles Olson

"*The whole thing: just trying to be at home. That's the plot.*"
—Robin Blaser

In ancient Judaic mystic traditions, scholars read the second letter (ב) of the Hebrew Aleph-Bet as reflection, medium—a connection between antecedence and expression, origination and articulation. Resembling a tent on a landscape, Bet is the first character in the Torah ('Beresheet': in the beginning). Beit, a derivation, means a measure, a home that comes before and goes on after one.

I.

Merkavah (Chariot Scene)

"To go before the ark...
as those who reach down into themselves
in order to perceive the chariot."
                —Gershom Scholem

                                Call it cavelight
                        unlike night—being, as I've wanted
                    myself to be, leaves the wind moves
                its summer teeth between—*you heed less*
    than you think you heed—I see nothing
                but the comfort of sunflowers
                    wilderness as comportment
                        even in darkness—*ophanim*
                                Not like it didn't take a lifetime
                    to be here—*sunflower blindness*
                        stained-glass language
                                of the vision
                        that defies us—wheels
                within wheels, the world
        wears the color of the spirit
                step lively
                    through
                        it

Swoon, in Blue (3)

Ocean green   chain of leaves
     handing down the willow tree—
   where your eye falls in strokes—dizzying
that night I bought a ring—   & ever since you can hear cicadas
     in the lightning crease—in the far corner   *real moss*

....

   not make believe

Floored by *newgrowth*

           evergreen forest rows   driven up the hillside—*this new life*

       you just feel a part of— thinking about the fire—

          this, that   was always

    the undisturbed rankness of—   embers in the sweet air—

the first of many visions

                ensembling

....

       Just a feeling

           ahead of evening: *so pretty*

   reigning in

       the eaves—

And because your head is full of bells

you live well—with your mistakes   your whole life   in the shape they take

three red flowers   unfolding   reasons for emptying   perfect if you

let it be a song on a train   in the morning—if you're ready

for cornflowers, say

....

all my days   *yes*

Happy just

       overheard music

    out of nowhere—voices out of time—immemorial—cathedral—spire

           where I first found your hand

      outside myself   for a moment—

....

      Fountain shade

         in the *Fontaine*

no particular way

         de Medici

      whosoever loves

a parade

      knows the future

waves overlapping

        always

      do you

say yes

      yes yes you say

Trees May Have a Heartbeat So Slow We Never Noticed
(New Scientist)

That was the headline today
and then the men came
with axes and saws—I came home
to bundles of limbs scattered across
the complex parking lot, cut off
at all angles, rough, too much to stuff
into dumpsters, so left there
drying in the desert sun.
So yes I have broken down
at Yad Vashem too many times
to count, seen too many mountains
baggage, glass, shoes—
piles of almost anything
undo me. My grandfather
from Lodz, my grandmother
Sephardi. Later after dinner
(it was Friday) I saw a blur circling
outside the window, helplessly. Have you ever
seen a hummingbird become confused? The soul
in my chest in that moment—I felt the wind move
boughs, traced out the cost of our greed—as branches
rise at night, the same way we might
see, after prayer, eyes downcast
for so long, the sun, like the first time
so personally involved in humanity
or rather, humanity like trees—

a trope that itself invokes the ideal
we imagine—branch sets
inspirited by dream
this part it seems
harder to explain—
how in crux, in crisis, we
ask after inheritance
interwoven in helix, as though
life was only our experience—our expertise
only do they, the branches, the terror
feel, the surge of forces for which they also
have no words? Tonight I watched my daughter
fall asleep. The rain fell red and apocalyptically
in the desert. I saw the day shatter breathless
no utter regard for me—at first
I questioned the art and then the body
then thought O god so
quietly

Fog

If I could only get out from under
for one minute, this fog
of responsible business
I know I could recover
the sound
sinewed around
this house unchanged
as echo original remains—

      north lighthouse   horn

          south lighthouse   horn

cannonfire—   there are others

hymns off-shore   in the grey middle din unintelligible

like shapes out of the mist   ships at first

then not at all like ships

      I mean I was in it

          when the fog rolled in

the milkwhite room—so easy to be

          found wanting

      walking without the right

          neighborhood signs

      in the street—ghosts of

          something major

      weighed in

      the balance—an idea really

          at stake—me

      with my stupid little book

drawing on such obvious things—in danger

          only of forgetting

the frontier line, not listening

    when the thrush birds speak—

in danger of not speaking myself

    where I stand, not recognizing

      the going home

  of sticks and stones and hands held out

        across tables—I mean I *felt* it

time wrapped around

    the worry—*time to make good*

on all the promises—spookily

    had my way

obscured by intention—

  wish I had wanted

so futile of me

   this sense of history—

There was a day

    with glass and

wind—felt beneath the lamplight then

  the crack of new beginnings

      zone of color arching the sky—

Someone shattered

the vessels of the universe

   with light. I remember

being so young and over

   hearing little switches

below the leaves

   make them start

stop shivering

Truces (for Tome)

"And the sea changes
Despite the poet it is next to."
—Jack Spicer

I know

about the truces now

after you have gone

how everything is on

TV at the right time

my life changes suddenly

the leaves fall anytime

not when they're called

and best of all I can be

given, not given

worry about the visions

anymore. Your siren song

stayed true—enough

in a letter that begins

dear, swift-flying apocalypse—

that you'll never send

another, that you

always meant to

me future, perfect

brave and blushing

fool exactly as I admire

I still long to be. Pray for détentes

you cannot sign—each a crackling

of happiness pointed at me, a spear

like Giacommetti's mobile in Paris,

Apollinaire's face in the window, my first

time really seeing the signs

for *Alcools* in the street—prophetically

what your voice brings up *(lost)*

as sometimes I forget

all my dread *(my as-yet*

mistakes), late flights

hospital beds, every time

you said   *don't fuck with me*

in the streets of Tel Aviv

getting pizza at midnight—

I remember this so clearly,

your cool, command

of all the hidden words, what might

only now, in my after life, get called *sublime*

acquiescence, all broke-up. Ahead

we move for lakes

for Galilee of hopes

parting might restore us—you

to your gardens, tuned to the lyres

for companions' passage

newly to arms, all love, we rest

desperately fronting closure as if

anyone felt ok. It didn't go that way—

I never could summon all your forms

least of all in the poem, and so remain

reaching ever after like branchlings

in a storm. What turns out

to be at stake in all this gasping—the world

we mistake as a place to hold our cares, faults

days—everyone we starch ourselves for

and to endure—*if only*

       you'd met my daughter—

and so much more. In that thought

I'm attendant again, like a gift you said

and a curse. A walking version

of Keats' "forlorn"—*tolled back to*

my sole self—at the races once more

paying poorer attention

no less anxious, aware

too much of east-facing siding

when the bills come due. I wasn't always like this

high up in your room. The heart in

my chest—do you remember

Ishmael in the crow's nest? How we used to laugh

off the cruelty of the world? In that compliment

of living must dying needfully be—lines written

in Thoreau's back pages—*outbound ships*

detained no more—as if it were possible

for you to come home. I mean

what's knocked your hate

into the creek lately? Can't you rend

the sky? You'd joke and say I wasn't there

at last for the breathing

the whole tide my body

won't give up—*you know this*

word, catharsis, eddy?—this evening's amorous

stance toward reality? Storm clouds

so loud, so count

myself lucky. And you

would be right—enough

to change. Peace to breath

every morning

the selfsame parade

all readymade

a freshet, a story, an eye

well on its way. Enough. You'd love it. I swear

the season cheers me, the second person

is always a ghost, and I miss you

each day all year. There are secrets

objects share—you

showed me—struck

by a heavenly

force of a like

kind, the needle

loses bearing—never

recovers—your heart

     in a field

of lightning kneeled

     of needs
you said
     no different

Lore

Just look
              at the light
of this hour—lore

of headstones, rooftops

the way antennae arrange

through chimneystacks

real ocean masts

the birds know at last

                    we can't stay
in alleyways

the next horizon already

underway. We can't leave either

our beautiful faces—so urgency

so color already

in pinwheels, increased

day by day. I had wanted to

show you an opening

in attention, a way

in the world arranged

toward happy-making—real

as it is to me, fields

of my family, finally

all I had asked for, singing

         and I
  was lightly
        at sleep

at everything

Association

It was summer
      and we all were

evacuating, because
      apartments

went to fire—that we might
      get filled up again

by something else,
      kenotic—we remembered

the feeling—what Levi
      and Derek were drinking

by the big blue bear
      in Denver, not so long ago

all clear—to become vision
      while falling. It's not sad

I was alone and kept calling out
      for you, even if I didn't

know the names yet. There
      are days

I go on because
      I go—you asked me

once what was at stake
      when I got what

I wanted, and framed
      in another door, I sang

these mountains—that you can see them
      such oasis
            in the desert
a heart can become

Elegy (Deserted)

"Hope: the following page. Do not close the book."
"I have turned all the pages of the book without finding hope."
"Perhaps hope is the book."
        —Edmond Jabés

We live on
      the edge of
A raft through
      dejection

A joy almost
      too great
To speak, so
      it takes

Breath,
      so we break
At the end
      of the line

Whenever we see the sun
      go on
The entire Death
      Valley covered

In a carpet of yellow
      and gold
pinafores. And you can't
      imagine the hills

Any more than
      deny
The contours
      the failing

Light that gives
      every angle
A vision
      as it goes

Froid (Aeolian Harp)

The wind tunes us
like backglances
between musicians
in the street
my love
say *eyes*
say *ruffian*
thick vines
of kudzu
struck by unending
light, always setting
things right, rough hewn
as we were back then
the sacred heart
we saw through
glass doors, finally home
in a world so made
a million paper cranes
on the way up, utterly
uncommon snow birds aloft—O
dear there is nothing left
on the rooftops for us
to apologize for

II.

Second Home (Bet)

I stood in the elevator, mirrored

                        on four sides   by the start of a new life

              and took stock of my hands—*beresheet*

    I counted all the chimney masts   on the Holocaust memorial school

        across the snowed-in avenue—brought home bread in the morning

found my way back out of the woods   I had built

                and lost myself   in saying

     be ok

. . . .

    and there

      were you

Happy just   electric

        beginning   out of nowhere   *that there is always*   *another dawn*

   risen   *on mid-noon, and under every deep*   *a lower deep opens—*

                          if only for one more moment

              in the park outside Shakespeare & Co.

      I'd take it—

....

         long enough with you to know

it isn't me   really   making this minute   holy. Thankfully

No ideas but—outside in the sky it's clear

just like this   chorus behind us   happy just to see

uneven fence posts before collapsing   the world makes sense again—young

          people always laughing   at the edge of death

....

          missing/not missing   everything

—and so it goes   morning makes it known   *move your hand*
     through the light   *and see flags—*   a parade
     drawn no particular way   a celebration   of leaves
                                        overlapping

....

                         childhood
                                   patterns sidereal
          always
                    good news—ever
                              lasting *I will*
          always love you

Be Ok O Hell

Be anywhere—living
proof emerged though
another kind of day
so springtime
revivifying
really there for us
like you were always
            light-tassled evergreen
newgrowth from the beginning
if you could say that
in a poem—*sunflower blindness*
unheard of—how could I
live without it? What couldn't we
do? I couldn't move
when I heard the news, like
I'd only just noticed
The year gorging itself on poets

The year gorging itself on poets

The year   still gorgeous

The noise of it

Ode on a Boson

The world isn't less
beautiful, it just
weighs more—the ocean
was always a place
to disappear—dance
swaying under bulb glass
saying always be
impressive, leave
early, everyone
in my generation
called dibs

—

During a difficult series
of months, scientists discover
the first shadow of an atom—you
go to a party, everyone
is a confection, and a boson
gets shook up—*if feelings*
can do that to the treetops
then what? Discovery
unsettling the wind, winnowing
every thought you thought
you'd need, like feathers—
          you were so happy
and so wrong, but so happy—enough
peace to breathe, gather
fireflies by the new river—leave
us here

Curvilinear

The leaves give the wind shape
to us, but are not
the wind itself, just
so, we call this
reading—flowers,
pitchers of light. Aren't they
       the whole world
started today—you can tell
by the parade. And some
of our grief. You can change
into fireflies anytime, streamline
toward the mountain

       transmitten eye

pull through laughter

       in the park recall

every day pianos start

       some *thing*

keeping the swarm aloft

       what *sun*—

That energy is our oarsman

Hekhalot 4

I loved bad paintings, door panels, set stages. Then dumplings, dead rabbits, and heaven
I loved a quiver   became a high-rise farm   and rafters   I tore
Tulips from the ground
Then nothing. Then
Tulips
....

—just like that. The world doesn't end, it hiccups. I break tea cups
in the kitchen till I feel better, listen to borrowed French records
bruised and drunk under the sun, I say *Dear Unimaginable*,
my heart forever

Dear Unimaginable: Phase Changes (Recovery)

Not like I didn't know it already—
past inclemency
and present warmth—like Hawthorne said—peeling like old pink
suitcases or your Cadillac
hips after three months in France—red birds
bent and pecking at the grass—negotiating my own salvation
against the body's stubborn insistence—to the end—hooked like this
sharp spiral staircase   by the taste of it—   two fountains, bright
streetlights   three, maybe four in the morning, all your shade
and sheet, in every corner, in the garden

....

Then grown
attuned
to handfuls of yellow
tea kettles in the window—*ancient light*
stinging nettle—the cold and lasting memory of
every talisman I ever loved
in the backseat of a VW—except the names
we saved for later—   Bach motifs—   the equator—
liquor, laughter, our daughter
news travels fast—
I'm hungry, I miss you, let's start

....

I am thinking now
of your gardens, civilization
through which passes
I imagine
all manner
of singing things
but not me. Not just yet
those of us
in need

most of dancing

or country. Ardor. Another

glass raising—*to be more*

than a signal—there's an art

to everything, someone

who saved my life

once said—resting

as well as resisting

I hear

the voice approach—

then again

the sun

has a voice too

so why not

let the gates of my chest

swing open

for a moment more

no violence

no harm done

the buffet

of the universe

adorned

with conversations

like you wouldn't believe

the sky moves

always, like new

listen, look you

might like it

Dear Unimaginable: Wake Today a Line

Famous
from abrogations
—should've seen it coming
all along, commotion
on the floor
the wanting more
than bells in the street—foolishly
stayed at the bar, devastatingly
wake and go outside today
on my bike. One fateful mistake
after another—lucky for
the line. Slouching toward Bethlehome, I find
little lists scattered throughout
the house, directions I didn't write
for future occasion—all by the light
and still somebody else has written   *cultivate/exalt*
on the side of a blue dumpster
in the alley behind the park   *I want to know*
the sun, each of the stars our own

Dear Unimaginable: Quies

The peace and sanity
           of a being that
no longer has to look
           at itself
           —

Sounds good, yes?
So called oblivious
Thomas Merton said
so grateful for this
morning after
the air   has substance
           you can feel it
when you go
the new world
shivers & pleats
life exists—you
can hear it
in the voice
and the hills—O
   them

Dear Unimaginable: Solstice in a City Full of Stars

For a while after I was rousted
around the house
differently, like an automaton
possessed by some
            other kind of light—

experience

    Spirit tells us

matters—everything
become firework
every where a very one
beyond measure
live & with music
plenty remains:
I fumble with apples
tomorrow the keys

Dear Unimaginable: Dum Spectas Fugio

Wednesday, the water is many
waves, and the lighthouse
has yet to remain
quiet. Today I helped a stranger
lug a Steinway down the stairs—
I know I can think about the melting
sea ice in my Collins glass
with the same language
as Greenland—all this
privilege, I do think about
Greenland a great deal—
is this the byproduct
of fatherhood? As much as the eye
is byproduct of the sun
        is light
on the rooftops in Connecticut
I felt all the hands, watched the listing
of newly bourn sea-crown ships   *I flee*
of spirits. Plenty remains. In need   *even as you observe me*
of advances rather than retreats—the wind
off the water moves differently
through three different trees. The point
is the island I am certain
halfway between my eyes
and the horizon
is real. And swiftly I guess
what the birds are
feeling—really different
outside the house
then in it

Dear Unimaginable: Portal (Wilder Shores of Love)

First heaven
        is all windows—*of course*
                I thought

everybody knows—
        you can see it
                in the evening

crest, the visibly rich
        old man at Brother's
                who spills his drink

on my notebooks
        so I look up
                and see the actual sun—

I have to go
        change my life
                again—so what

else is new, next—*There*
        is no end in nature, what
                Joshua Trees will believe

every time a universe explodes
        a chromosome knows
                to reassemble

for some reason
        I dream of your eyelashes
                again, Desi Arnaz

on an old neighborhood radio—
        the whole year
                ushering in

a jump right off
        into helplessness
                one after another, disabused

of intention. At a Cuban restaurant
for the love of—
wouldn't help to fake it

what little sense this makes—any poem
thrown on a landscape

the hearth of this

onward
movement
awake

Stillness/Forgiveness (Hekhalot 1)

Collar bone / Broken blinds / The sun, lousy with guilt
I am not afraid of being alone with you / Hung down
on ribbons / Aspens under tree houses, orange glowing
in my hands / In the park, crook of neck / A litany of
echoes in the timbers and the dump truck rattles
toothbrushes in the morning / On the news a Russian fire
burns half the churches in St. Petersburg / There is no one and
ash against ash against snow, street sweep, silver

There is a slow weary harvest in the fields / Swords into plowshares / The window son / Embellished in secret Overnight a cathedral / Rising freely / A way of seeing touches clearing / Do you not say *four more months and then the harvest?* Look / Three stones cut from the field

A look, shuddering / *Shook with mercy* / I found you two other oceans / A brown leather suitcase / No winnow to blossom / The sun / A mountain / *It's cold* / And a humid space / Cameras in the mirrors / Cinch the shutters / Eat the heart / *I can't believe he's not dead* / On the news two newlywed morning glories swallowed by a house / A house swallowed by a whale / A whale swimming alone in the ocean, holding its breath

Merkavah (Stepwell)

Thirteen boys walk up a mountainside, eleven walk down
A bird tries to fly but its wings are already on fire. And it was not a man
If you named the mountain, not the boys—the cliff, not
The trees. If somehow the way up did not have to mean *now*
The boulder. Six hours. Eleven boys. *I'd known my whole life*—and a helicopter
We build children of stone. Every book says so—thirteen boys take the shirts off
their backs, soak them in blood—a bird tries to fly but it is a man and

       we thought it was dead

    does not have wings

        already on fire

Four dozen archers nestled in a tower. A red jar in a kitchen footprints in a field of leaves. Shadowed, every night for twelve hundred, never coming home. And this is the story of..
....
...............*will hold you to the ends of the earth,* an airplane, and love does no good. There is a beach. And platforms connected by unstable bridging. Let's just say you see something on the beach. In the forest. *Why wouldn't you just say*...............love   will   pin   you   to   the   ends   of   the   earth   and
....

Hekhalot (Exit, Pursued by a Bear)

In a shallow, frozen creek: signs of   *chased into—*

fan the area   ferns and moss and rotting timbers   a dusting

of snow, aching, slippery, so rotten   *a family turns into a road*
          can't see, turns back. A man tries for the coast, but there's no—*something*

has to happen   something always does

Merkavah (Solomon Maps)

So much of what I had
        forgotten

Ancient maps
        of Antarctica

Before they could've been
        known

Laid bare upon
        seeing

I turned my eye
        around the thing

My daughter—
        I thought

Piri Reis
        Oronteus Finneus

And then what?
        Only beginning

I reckoned
        cold-front—

How will I
        drive the car?

A feeling left of
        what we can't

conceive—all that magic
        I have no defense

To believe
        still in the end

To simply
      have been

Here long enough
      to know

All that remains
      as furnace

Brilliance of fruit
      that makes

Something of sun
      its days

Hekhalot (Branch)

Such surprise cracklings
in the branches assert spring—I dream
a beautiful bird dissolving
any distinction between
means and message
in my mouth—*form*
        never more
than extension
of—bravery
I tell myself
is always original
the feeling changes
as if there weren't always people
in love, the way we get on
the train like nothing's
ever happened. *No harm*
done. Prospero again. Certainly
not in the asters, chandelier
constellations, the high
iron windows tonight—
this resemblance, that paradise
finds its parade
is all I ever needed
to know—every day
a new calling, so
I say something
unimportant, and you
say heart is the only whole
word—ok good. Just one look
and I'm buoyed
again, a winter
proposal, a garden brass
band, branches settling
into street lights
where and *when*

        your hand–

III.

Achilles Mourning the Death of Patroclus

"Our poems cannot live alone
any more than we can."
—Jack Spicer

It was time

that was the tenderness—still light yes

& all our breakfasts

at once—painting

alone now at home

I understand how

you became so sad—brushes so cold

I looked out at the snow—light—*still*

time adapts to the breathing

of the born and dying body—*a party*

you said—*enjoy*

every sand spit, landscape

strobe light, sandwich

across the street in abandoned complexes

bright colors dancing—so I stopped looking

for patterns in secret, opposite. For a moment

just kind of gave up on it

breaks my heart. Called this my life

and it turns green—

Alpenglow just before

and after passing. I know

I feel something circling

underneath every crow's nest

I go to sleep. Descartian vortices

coordinate wings—can't say

other than I mean—*I dreamt I saw you*

    in the back gardens

the day my daughter starts swaying

with the lyres—dancing

        white phosphorescent

    fine wires

my incorrigible shaking

mornings—a curse

and a prayer, built in

the interior. So thank you

no one tells you

you'd understand

the body confused

by breath at last—thought

for so long *my own*

proven so deftly

not so. This insistent

gift in us, breath

of transience, a daily kind

of echo, practice, promise

of real transgress—*fled*

is that music—and death

just takes your breath

because it obeys *rules*? We get it:

darkness waves & the unknown

fidgets. There remains in abundance

mysterium tremendum inside

every *sanctum sanctorum* and sometimes

even the hummingbirds stand still.

Certain things you have to be

this close to the animal

to understand. How a foal knows

to kick a menacing rustle, never

glimpsing danger before. The sun

or what is breaking in us. The language

of reeds, the way your body

lets go of me—the air in the room

echo too some far song

along series—what kills me

is our chances anyway

and the police, you'd say

catching my own reflection

in animistic totem

feeling lost and found

like home in the morning

like I've never known

danger at all—still green. No stopping

sublimating robins

in eastwardly siding—a whole

new day eloping—always

I'm still sorry—

Seriously. I wanted to tell you: All we have anymore

are welcome home parties. It's perfect

and sad. Every future

anew—we'll take it. *Hey, Achilles!*

It's ok. We've been waiting.

What cruelty

is of needs

must break

if in the line

if we—

given away

Hekhelot (Physical Laws)

Easier to say *I heard*

the new Tribe record today

and started crying—became a father, think O

God you would've loved this—

I thought
    speak

kindly enough
        to keep

the wilder parts
        intact

to remember us
        our youth

quit mistaking economy
        for a lifetime

what Williams called
        responsibility

laws for
      the lake—
so indifferently

angels to my mortgages
      as life to our mistakes

a spark in a break
      in searching

for a second
      becoming an act

of home come
      sprawling

the way color doubles
      over

the horizon—lily
      and cherry blossom

of darkness
      three flowers

in the cover
      where the eye

must go

First I Wanted to Be an Athlete

of God, then was

found wanting, then

wanting more—*love*

a republic   *if you can keep it*   a republic if not—   sacred enough
to be lost   in luster   either way, fanatical   windblown through evergreen
branch pews   as should be   still wholly   the sky   *tatterdemalion my*
tent against the—

not against

....

alongside

Merkavah (Apertures)

Wind proofs writ

larger than this

night sky my

daughter's enrapturer

stay awake call

by its name

any happiness

this very thing

a light like guilt

settles on joy if we

aren't vigilant

wooden window shutters on

open pin hinges

red roof tiles

with small black pigeons

a clearing in *park* while

new shadows find trees

maybe train tracks

some sometimes sounding geese

Radar Birds

"The point of no return was the beginning."
—Fleur Adcock

Or maybe they knew
they were needed—
millions of wings
coalescent in the curve
of tragedy—rapture into tantivy
murmuration scenes—awake
before the wake—maybe
they saw it coming
spooky patterning
the self couldn't shake
—can you imagine
—why do you think
starlings form
on the whole?
Minutes before
the trembling, hopefully
woven, the very fabric
of clarity—bodies in space
foretelling all told. What else
is vision but earthly
      faults awakening
all birds
      haunted on the radar
before the quake—
      slats of attention
the world avails, presaging
         the storm

Troglodytidae

"What must the winter wren be, then—
They say it is far ahead of this."
      —Walt Whitman

If you had to name *this*—

      Hole in what through which

....

a winter wren—
               gables covered
in grape vine and   organs playing
through which occasionally
               a distant sail—
youthful lasting   act of   aspen in autumn

brambles through fence lines—moving—faint yellow
windowsill through which—box elder—first signs of

hands and all

this clearing

Needs Work (Beresheet)

"What force unmoors my book, what light hails it?
I live among unrecognizable creatures.
The sun unwinds on a different continent."
—Edmond Jabès

What of mention doesn't
   save

the desert cactus
   bloom, the Wandering

Jew, the sun, its daily irruptions
   must

of needs be irrelevant,
   isn't it

heavenly, not
   wrong work

hailed as new, unkindness
   costumed

by finery, jealousy obscuring
   contours true

every shape walks through
   the world already

hierophantic so unto to the whole how
   add? Every body

says we have enough poems
   with birds in them

but who says

we have enough birds

or poems? Tracks left by deer in grass

thoughts through rain windows

tiny spiders little wires yellow-breasted

sun suddenly across the park come

these street lights, string trees

changing aspects of light

rocky hills flush with

leaves turning into tiny

birds entirely covering branches

Red 1

When we awoke
the sound: windswept—*as with any new word, where to begin?* We grew

to love it, and in between   felt stirring, something home like
the sun   in the desert   great providence   gifted   yellow diamonds
caught in a web   beneath a mountain   *you can hear them singing*
on the trail   a child says   *the ones you can't see*

Red 2

And taught to define a loss—

witness a desert city in a sandstorm—to insist   certain colors have real thirst
Freemont Cottonwood / Silktassel Bush   and move on   imagine what's at stake and all
     I could think was   *but wouldn't it be still glorious / to go out and throw my arms around*
an entire tabernacle of finches   one possible tree   dismantles the whole thing
        sudden portals of rain   when I look up
              from the book   just right   here, jubilant of birds

Red 3

To any that say *the mountain isn't vision*—who argue clouds
when you first walk in—all I see is the view
then everything through which you are better
is true. *You are beautiful, small springboard*
in the iris rhododendron
hedgerows, looking
for—well, fixing up
in the morning. A prayer
and a glass with a hand
to pour out the spirit—
good God enough
now for a minute
       dayenu /
           bevakasha

Hekhelot (Winter, NY)

Wind-watched

voice of

stillness—shifting lattice   waves pulled across

visible lake underside   sensible through trees

shiver

ever

green

every changing part of me

Arrow of green
      light broke up by redwood streams—opening
onto fir edge—thin lines, eddy breach, belief
      made entire of leaves—eyes
           not reluctant,
        mouth changed   by clear tidal waves—*to utter*
           anything hopeful—
        becoming of our names
           a haystack   outcropping of rock
              bored through by days
           just past which
                  a whole new
        entrancement begins

Riperian 2

Still encouraging
                              such brightness—
            always apocalyptic
near the ocean, if you're paying attention   break   into cloud arrays
            I still don't know what to say—I mean I was lost
                      then flailing then lost and found again
        and such abundance   *amidst abundance of pain*

....

So somnambulance   no more, I decided   not to invent new ways   to be injurious
      said   *don't interfere*   (gratefully)   called love harmonics   in waves
in what ways   we might   be patterns   (please)   never taught   to be
 but true   accept   let go find   the heart
     that polymath   who knows what bright   disturbance
this wind   again might be   absolving us

Auberge

—like oranges

swaying from every tree, lyre

strings plucked in pageantry

engaged with the world we were

meant to be—carried

home on bright distances, wings

I remember seeing foolish, newly

full of greeting, every window recently

become my life. I believed my father, still

listen to the night relief

—*that was my story.* A way in

through which with all the vibrations

of *jaune*, summer, something

pacific and squalorous

might remain. Relinquishing

home, I called the song

scaffolding, went about my business

climbing fences, listening to *ouseau*

unfold in breath. It was delight

bade my days, the way cobalt

unsteadying arranged—*could be*

raining, certainly feels choppy in the deep—

first lights far off on the Jetty

frozen at the sight

of a spiral I hadn't

imagined—a flock

of a sudden, visible clouds

sidereal, astral under eaves, all over

with my body—*H sticks out*

one foot from under the blankets—and the storm

of my life tunes up. Every lamp I see

across the street: my eyes

       stay struck with you forever—

the way color doubles over

       the horizon, we say *breathing*

is hard when we feel

       most alive—what must one be

but dancing? Only answer

       I've arrived at

worth satisfying

The Difference Between a Poison and a Food

That one kills you

     and the other does not is not

the point really a question rather of what

     and what you do with it yes but O then what a wretch

was I not so long ago without a thought of dying

     —did I deserve to know oblivion the horizon then

        drunk up by sky always a line worth crossing love

     was always a kind of drink for me of many for a time

this much I can say and that I did love too much yes

     but not in the way I do now O now that the aspens quake

       in unison outside today being of one

     perfect chorus, form, affection, animal eye, addiction

        more than stifles such solace

and still it matters, this fading light on my favorite

       album cover—one single branch

        like the feeling the next one

         might redeem

      me, if only I keep traipsing

        up the next nick of time

      O time might fix me

Day Without Pain

The wind moved the trees
today—I can't explain
any other way—in the coming
storm, some of us called
it plain, the rest
learned to behave
precisely as aubade—
    to get through it
again—I recalled the garden and
the desert it became. Together
we did our best to stay
the redshift of days. It worked
for a time, our brightness
rang out fields of white lilies
into the half moon bay.
That was love
regardless of taxonomy
what anyone says
is family
is never the all
of it. The old house
became a good new show—
a life when I looked up, foundling
alongside the most elegant sentences
I didn't have to imagine
remaining, and I've stayed
shattered ever since
by the concision
of each consequent
movement the light
today through
our kitchen rakes

American Dream

I will stand up straight
in the mirror
give the succulents
what they've always been
asking for—I will
repopulate courage
in the space left
inside my breast—I promise
evincing an absolutely
modern sense
of abandonment
one great pine epic
never gave up on me
I've been backed by a quiver
of stars since morning
it's a whole new time of year

First Heaven

"Better get out of town
before your nickname expires."
—Warren Zevon

How paradise
finds its parade—
the way you sang
in Spain before anyone
was there, and the light
behind the pianos
I swear I saw
the thing itself
for once and all
tiny and star-lined
out-of-pocket
blindness infinite like
Blake said windowed
with interrelatedness
of everything
that touches
some cell else
and all the day
goes on in color
with or without us
and also the sun
I swear I haven't seen
this before
such new twist
of marble moved
around the run—
Something didn't want me

forgetting such

feeling—*when*

Johnny strikes up the—

calico blue sky

outside, air

conditioner

your best

riot of spirit

any minute now

the whole swell of it

good god it

was perfect

Antinomianism

"I desire that place might be answered."
—Anne Hutchinson

I didn't realize
the rules don't change
I thought I knew the name
love never called itself
one thing only and weakness
and habit make it harder—*go bother*
          your fuzzy head
about God—
cloud visions tilting
off the topside
of buildings instead
of the reflection
of your face
in a town center
window barraged and
arranged by branch sets
the way faith and affection
rattle a spiral out of us
shake loose the spirit
from fear, if only for
a beat, if only
abeyance
once to stop
the ghost ship's
dazzling hooks
to set in

America Windows

*"Why should not our nests be as interesting things
to angels, as bullfinches' nests are to us?"*
—John Ruskin

Blood iron patina—
weathering
constellation body   of plains, affection   cramped up together   on a train
     lenticular frames   withering   *is this of what life is   yet made*—whatever
the difference between echoes remains   and choices   the line between the   between
               history of—   attached to bone   alone, spirit but no—
every character knows—*bad things will come of this*—wood sign, wood smoke *what
     exactly is it they're getting away with*—sign reads: *Amos's Redemption Center*
                    just before   and after thick consumption
                         arranged beautifully
                         bridging between
....
     white   green   calf-tall   tan   fields   of wheat

Passion
                    built in the procession of—

shapes in the verdure—branchlings—tight-pointed apocrypha—high-tipped

with spade leaf, bell tower, meanings   grown in another book—*I didn't write*
            the train stops   because the bridge is up
the train stops us   because   *slow black cyclone of birds*
            played-out sun   startling over fields—*what do you think happens*
    in those woods?
....

A creek where one shouldn't be—as if there were ever such a thing—space cleared
out by someone in trees—the middle of nowhere is *never*—broken up windows
arranging the sun
                                            on the company side of town—facsimile
    warehouses, except where ivy on brickframe irrupts—cultivated decay, fooling
                exactly nobody
half-hearted scrawl on the side of a Cross-Fit near an American flag just says
Phantom Kings
                                        praying mantis
                                                clouds orchestral

                        back of the whole thing

That I have learned to read the veins
                        on the back of my hand   last
made for difficulties   like leaves
                    in the bottom of a glass—I understand:
                                        to keep in touch—
I tell my grandfather this   this morning   because as a scientist   I imagine
            he'll understand   the thermodynamics   of my failing
over the phone—   because he is dying   and I'm not home—strong winds
            standing space up—   against nothing—   purple cattails

                    beer trash trail, grass, green

                                        perfection forever

            thrown up
        to heaven—purple cattails
....
    still hope
                incarnate contrails

sanctifying each
            and every sky

A shockingly blue shtetl—a mother, moon, muddy river bottom—I imagine my origins—and the light
    falls through—*bayberry   briar path   salt spray rose   beech forest   blossom*   the point
was always the music   was there for us—light   let in through degrees—like
    the way stains in the scene break   alongside rain—it *is a beautiful world*—you get a second
to yourself   and the view   resounds   off every infinity room. I miss you. Really you
··
                                                    do become
                        each blessing past the window—
    Your love becomes the view. Awes in *if you're not careful*. I sit in the chair and don't
die. Skies move
                                                            crazy, crazy
                                            true—

Iowan river water
                    runs right off the edge of
perception—*this close to heaven*
wind must be, my daughter says to me, as my notes blow away into the stream
—the word *powers*—I watch the waves the same way I said my vows—*unexpected*
wind trailing through trees—it's not that it makes me better, this view
of the woods, what it affords, not that I am asking it to,
asking after needs, but deeper, unto the whole how
fast
          grey finches

Beit

To call home
>this second

act of becoming
>whole, moveable—*feast*

your eyes—there
>*shall be no rust*

on the gates of—this

I have learned. Surviving
>any thing matters

Staying related
>to the beyond

but lovingly, *the world wears*
>*the colors of*—

Not to invent
>mistakes to make

good on all
>the promises, hands held out

across tables, *non tableaux*, and heart
>without saying, go—

the bartender whispers
>*trop froid*—

so we all fall

>in love

with the day

>the world

so made

      the way

it remains

      you can stand by

a parade

      when it tilts

or saunters, really

      points to relief—it's not like

we're not bereft

      already, like the barge

of our sorrows

      hasn't set—and yet

have you seen the lights

Notes

"Merkavah (Chariot Scene)" engages phrases from Emerson's *Nature* and C.D. Wright's *Deepstep Come Shining*.

"Truces (for Tome)" contains language from Thoreau's *Journal*.

"Lore" opens with Robert Creeley's headstone.

"Froid (Aeolian Harp)" quotes Coleridge.

"Second Home" includes a selection from Emerson's essay "Circles."

"Dear Unimaginable: Phase Changes (Recovery)" quotes Carl Phillips.

"Dear Unimaginable: Quies" begins with a quote by David Jasper.

"Hekhalot (Branch)" quotes Charles Olson quoting Robert Creeley.

"Achilles Mourning the Death of Patroclus" quotes Warren Zevon and John Keats.

"First I Wanted to be an Athlete" quotes Benjamin Franklin and Donald Revell.

"Needs Work (Beresheet)" works with *The Book of Questions* by Edmund Jabès, and is inspired by Emily Dickinson.

The "Red" sequence employs variations on Cole Swenson's *Book of a Hundred Hands*, Lorine Niedecker's *Next Year,* and takes its title from Anne Carson. "Antinomianism" contains language from C.D. Wright's poem "Shallcross," from Jack Spicer, and the trial of Anne Hutchinson.

Acknowledgements

Grateful acknowledgement is made to the following journals in which some poems previously appeared, often in alternative formats and under different titles: *Colorado Review, Interim, Academy of American Poets, Conduit, Sixth Finch*, and *Everyday Genius*. Special thanks to Don, Geoff, Kathryn, Brenda, Andy, Colby, Oscar, and—more than anyone—Hanna, for taking care of these pieces when they needed it. Love is a lighted view you show ever anew.

The following poems are in dedication—

Swoon, in Blue (3) is for Hanna
Lore is for Bob
Association is for Geoff and Kathryn
Second Home (Bet) is for Aya
Be Ok O Hell is for C.D.
Curvilinear is for John
Dear Unimaginable: Phase Changes (Recovery) is for Paris
Dear Unimaginable: Dum Spectas Fugio is for James
American Dream is for Don
First Heaven is for Warren

Photo by Hanna Andrews

Eryn Green's first book, *Eruv*, was selected by Carl Phillips as the winner of the Yale Series of Younger Poets Prize, and was published by Yale University Press in 2014. Of his work, *Publishers Weekly* has written, "When touched by Green's gaze, the world teems with meaning," and *Christian Science Monitor* says, "The writing here demands one's full concentration, but gives a lot in return." Eryn's poetry, prose, and non-fiction has been featured in *The New York Times, Colorado Review, Denver Quarterly, Interim, Conduit, Painted Bride Quarterly, jubilat, Esquire*, and elsewhere. Currently an Assistant Professor in the English Department at the University of Nevada, Las Vegas, where he teaches creative writing, mythology, and coordinates the World Literature Program, Eryn lives near the Red Rock Canyon Conservation Area with his wife and daughter.

Editor's Choice

2019: Eryn Green
BEIT

2018: Rebecca Dunham
Strike

2017: Todd Fredson
Century Worm

2016: Matthew Minicucci
Small Gods
Mark Irwin
A Passion According to Green

2015: Claire Bateman
Scape
David Blair
Arsonville

2014: Adam LeFevre
A Swindler's Grace
Myronn Hardy
Kingdom
Jennifer K. Sweeney
Little Spells

2013: Judy Halebsky
Tree Line

2012: Cullen Bailey Burns
Slip
Katie Peterson
Permission

2011: David Keplinger
The Most Natural Thing
Mark Irwin
Large White House Speaking